CW00499168

A Tiger Bay Childhood

Growing up in the 1930s

ISBN 1-898317-04-6

Typeset: Marco A Gil-Cervantes
Cover Design: Bev Morgans
Illustrations: Olwen Blackman Watkins
Art Reproduction: Athena Repro Ltd
Printed: British Gas, Wales

A Tiger Bay Childhood
Growing up in the 1930s

Phyllis Grogan Chappell

ACKNOWLEDGEMENTS

To all the staff and volunteers of the Butetown History & Arts Centre.

To British Gas, Wales for their invaluable support in the printing of this book.

To the Arts and Libraries Committee of South Glamorgan County Council for the funding to ensure this publication.

And last, but very far from least, to Bob Chappell for his patience at my frequent absences whilst this book was in preparation!

CONTENTS

PREFACE

This is not the story of my life. It is simply a record of memories of a childhood spent "Down the Docks" in Cardiff. Some of the sights and sounds, the smells, the feelings.

Father Garland and Father Thomas in their soutanes and birettas; the slow, stately processions around St Mary's Church with the Vicar in his embroidered robes swinging the fragrant smoking censer, the choirboys following in their white surplices; the mild eyes of Miss Planck, one of my teachers interned in the War because she was German; Auntie Doris' giggle; "Oh for the Wings of a Dove", "The Teddy Bears' Picnic" and "Red Sails in the Sunset" on old wax records. Washing day (always Monday) and the smell of steam and wet cloth when we came home from school at dinner time; Nana's own smell when she held me close on her lap talking to whoever was on the other side of the fireplace; the smell of the Bute Street chemist with the great coloured glass jars in the window where we would be sent to buy honey as a treat for tea. Yes! honey was bought in a chemist's shop in those days! The smell of school, chalky, dusty, bringing a chill feel to my stomach! the feel of the hands of other children as our hands touched in games, some hands already rough from lighting fires and doing housework in their homes; the scratchy, horrid feel of long woollen stockings especially after they were washed!

Enjoy the book. It may bring back memories to those of you who lived through the same times with me. It might help those younger to understand how we lived in the "olden days".

1

Chapter One

MY FAMILY, MY WORLD

The first of my ancestors to arrive in Cardiff was my great-great-grandfather, one John Evans. He came to Cardiff from Bristol with his wife, Hannah, and a son, William. Two more children were born in Cardiff, a son, John, and a daughter, Mary (born 1842). The Evans family lived in Herbert Street. I am descended from Mary.

John Evans Senior, was a block and pump maker who exported his goods to the Continent. Presumably, he also sold locally.

John Evans

His daughter, Mary, was given an education which included French. As a young woman, she wrote and translated her father's foreign correspondence for him.

John Evans' wife died when Mary was a teenager and he went on to marry his wife's maid, who must have been in her twenties. That was all of the story that my generation was told. Recently, however, since I have been researching the family history, I have discovered that they had a daughter, Lucy. This fact was never mentioned by later generations, so I suppose it must have been something of a scandal at the time — John being around sixty and his wife being thirty or more years younger and being the maid. I would dearly like to know what became of Lucy and if there were any more children of this marriage.

In 1861 Mary married a young man, Alfred Budding, who lodged in a nearby house. Alfred was born in Gloucestershire. His family seems to have lived in that area for generations.

From the marriage of Mary and Alfred five children were born. The second child, Hannah Louisa, born in 1864, became my grandmother.

Alfred Budding died in 1882 and some years later, at the age of forty-four, Mary married again. Her second husband was Thomas Peach Houseley, who also had five children. Thereafter the two families — the ten children plus the two adults — lived all together as one household.

Hannah was the only girl in the family, having four brothers. She used to tell us that she had to fight to maintain her position amongst the four boys.

One of those boys became a policeman in Bristol but I don't know what happened to the others. I remember two of them when I was a child visiting our house regularly. They were charming, rosy-faced old men who would give me and my brother threepence or sixpence each and pat our heads.

Hannah did not have much schooling. In those days schooling had to be paid for and the school she occasionally attended cost 1d (old pence — a fraction of today's penny) a week. If her mother did not have the penny to give her Hannah did not go to school. Consequently she did not learn to read as a child.

Hannah was sent out to work when she was about twelve years old. Like many other working-class girls, she "went into service." That is, she became a servant in the homes of better-off people.

Alfred Budding

Mary Budding (nee Evans) and Thomas Peach Housley, her second husband.

Nana (Hannah) told us one or two tales of her days in service. One such tale was about the vicar who starved his children. She felt sorry for them, so when the vicar went out she would cook them meals.

There was also the tale about the mistress in Llandaff whom my Nana had to accompany to Llandaff Cathedral on Sundays, carrying a lantern to light the way if it was dark. Like other servants who accompanied their masters and mistresses, Hannah was not permitted to attend the service. Servants had to stay in the porch and wait until the end of the service and then accompany their employers back home.

On one occasion Hannah, having taken her mistress to church, skipped off to see her boy friend, who was the son of the station-master at Llandaff Station. Time must have passed very quickly because by the time she got back to Llandaff Cathedral everyone had gone home, including her mistress (who had no lantern, Hannah having it with her). The mistress had to make her way home in the dark across fields and on the way walked into a donkey who must have set up a loud braying. The poor woman almost had a fit — she thought the devil had come to take her off! Hannah wasn't sacked but her ears burnt for days after.

Hannah also had a lot of cautionary tales for us when we were small children. There was the naughty little child who *would* put her table knife in her mouth and run away from her nurse who was trying to make her take the knife out. In the middle of one such caper, the child fell and cut her mouth and died! Then there was the naughty little boy who was too greedy. Having pushed too much food into his mouth, he choked. Finally, of course, we were reminded of the poor starving children in Africa when we wouldn't finish our dinner.

There were stories as well of April Fools' Day when the newest and most innocent staff member would be sent on an errand to buy or borrow some impossible and non-existent article. He would be sent to a neighbour who, realising the joke, would send him on to a further neighbour who would send him on further and so on until the poor boy finally realised he was being duped.

At the age of twenty, which would be in 1884 or '85, Hannah Louisa Budding (later to be my Nana) met Andrew McCluskey, a Canadian seaman born in Nova Scotia.

Andrew came from a fishing family and when he was about fourteen years of age his parents put him into a monastery to become a monk and one of his sisters into a nunnery. Andrew was unable to stand the life and eventually ran away to sea arriving after one of his voyages in Cardiff where he saw Hannah sitting on the banks of the Glamorganshire Canal enjoying the summer air and went up and spoke to her; eventually they married.

After settling in Cardiff Andrew returned at one time to Canada to find his sister but was never able to do so. Presumably the rest of the family was scattered, as he never saw them either.

The day before they married Andrew asked Hannah to go to the theatre with him but her mother would not allow her out to go to such a place and locked her in her bedroom at the back of the house. Hannah (who had fought all her brothers at a younger age!) was not daunted. She waited for her mother to go back downstairs and then opened the window and climbed out on to the outhouse and so down and over the garden wall and on to the theatre! This was in the days of crinolines so it must have been quite a sight.

Andrew and Hannah married when she was twenty and he a few years older but their married life was not very long.

Andrew died of bronchitis at the young age of thirty-five, leaving Hannah with five children of whom the third, Mary Eleanor (Polly), was my mother.

The father's death had a great effect on the family. At the time of his death the eldest daughter, Eliza, was nine years old. She was taken from full-time schooling to look after the younger

7

Hannah Louisa Budding and Andrew McCluskey.

children while their mother went out to work.

The school they attended was in Mount Stuart Square in the north corner, backing on to the canal. Polly used to meet a friend outside the school every day and they would go in together. One morning Polly was waiting as usual but her friend did not turn up. Polly waited a while and then went to look for her friend. There was a path through to the canal and it was this way that her friend usually came so Polly went down that path to the canal bank. And there she found her friend — in the canal "with her long hair spread all around," as Polly used to say when she told the story. The poor child was dead — drowned. Polly attracted the attention of some men who were working on the canal who then came and brought the child out. Years later Polly would weep as she related this incident.

Andrew McCluskey (in dark coat, holding cross). The church is believed to be St Mary's, Bute Road, or St Michael's.

Hannah McCluskey at the wedding of the son of her employer, who owned an Hotel in Llandaff. Hannah, sitting furthest right of the picture, has been celebrating too enthusiastically and is very happy!

Eliza went to school only part-time after the death of their father and left school for good at the age of eleven to find work at Del Guerra's making oilskin garments. Polly managed to get another year at school, leaving at the age of twelve.

The young Polly became a tailor's apprentice, working for a Cardiff tailor. She began by running errands and tidying the work room. (The older girls would send the youngsters out for snacks, tea and so on.) Then she progressed to "ripping": that was removing the tacking stitches from clothing that had had the

Mount Stuart Square School: Polly McCluskey, front row, second from right.

Mount Stuart Square School: Polly McCluskey, back row, third from left.

11

Mount Stuart Square School: Alfred McCluskey, back row third boy from left.

Polly McCluskey

Alfred McCluskey

permanent stitching put in. She went on to stitching on gold braid — on to naval uniforms — and eventually to every aspect of tailoring. That is, she eventually became a proper tailoress.

At the time of the expulsion of the Jews from Russia a number of refugees came to Cardiff. Some of them went to work at the tailor's shop with Polly and her colleagues, and she made

Louisa McCluskey

friends amongst them (I can't bring any names to mind now). She and her sisters were teased because their name ended with "skey." "They must be Russian," people said.

One of the younger daughters, Louisa, died at the age of nineteen from consumption (tuberculosis) — another death which had a lasting effect on the family. Louisa was still talked about in my lifetime as if she had died only yesterday.

Hannah's eldest son, Alfred John, ran away from home at the age of fourteen and went to sea (following in his father's footsteps). He eventually arrived in Australia, where he jumped ship and stayed. He worked at various jobs, from sheep farming to goldmining and coasters around Australia.

At the age of twenty six, Mary Eleanor McCluskey (i.e., Polly), married Henry James Ambers, aged twenty three. Henry, the eldest of thir-

*Florence Ambers, with her
youngest daughter, Brownie
(Marguerite)*

*Polly in Ramsgate with Harry's two youngest sisters, Brownie
(Marguerite) and Norah.*

14

Mary Eleanor McCluskey, aged 18, wearing her Confirmation dress (made by herself).

teen children, was born in Ramsgate in Kent. I have been unable to trace his ancestry far back but the family descended from a French immigrant a couple of generations ago. (I am trying to find out more.) His father, Henry Bates Ambers, was born in Bermondsey, London, as was his mother, Florence Eleanor Grogan. Henry Bates Ambers' father was Frank Ambers, a seaman. The parents of Florence Eleanor Grogan were Harriet (née Buckingham) and James Grogan who had been a bandsman in the 11th Hussars.

Henry left home as a boy to join the army, which he eventually had to leave on grounds of invalidity. When the Great War started in 1914 he wanted to rejoin the army, which I suppose wouldn't have him because of his having been invalided previously. In order to return to the army, he changed his surname, using his mother's maiden name of Grogan. He went by this latter name for the rest of his life — which is how my maiden name ended up being Grogan instead of Ambers.

My parents, Mary and Henry, met and married during the Great War. However, they had no children until first my brother, Francis Henry, was born in 1928 — followed by me shortly thereafter. I was born in 1930 in North Church Street, the street which formed the boundary at the top of Tiger Bay.

Henry James Ambers-Grogan and Mary Eleanor McCluskey, probably on their wedding day.

16

The church in North Church Street was St Mary's, which is still there although the street has long gone. There was also a South Church Street and a Greek Church Street. Greek Church Street is named for the Greek Orthodox Church which still is in it — just behind the Salvation Army and the People's Dispensary for Sick Animals now.

Bute Road was and is a long straight road — one mile long people used to say. Whether that is true I don't know: maybe it just looks like a mile long.

Tramcars used to clash, lurch, grind and clatter up and down Bute Road — their destinations being Roath Park, Victoria Park and the Royal Oak. The Pier Head was the beginning and end of the known world then. So all the trams started from there and went all over the town. They were like great metal galleons hurtling (not really but they made so much noise that it seemed so!) along the roads, heaving to and fro as they went.

The seats inside the tramcars were all made of wood. Downstairs there was a long seat going the whole length of the car on either side. Up the twisting staircase at each end of the car you came to the upper deck which had seats laid out in pairs on either side in the same manner as buses nowadays — except that these seats were wooden and the backs were made of metal bars with wooden tops and could be pushed to and fro so that you could sit facing the front or the back of the tramcar.

There were stairs at both "the front" and "the back" of the tram. "Front" and "back" are in quotation marks here because, depending on which direction the tram was going, either end could be facing forward they could be driven from either end as some trains can today. In any event, at either end of the tram, as you came up the stairs and turned around, there were two long seats facing each other along with a narrow sliding window at the corner of the car. Children would always hang out of this window, until they were hauled back by their parents or some other difficult adults!

The Bay was said to be a violent place. I did not find it so. However, I did once see a knife-fight. I was walking down the Bay, to where I don't remember. I turned a corner and there were about half a dozen men, knives in their hands, stalking round each other and occasionally diving towards each other. I moved — fast! — back in the direction from which I had come. I didn't stop running until I arrived back home!

There was another occasion when I was sent by a teacher to ask why one of my classmates had not arrived at school. The girl in question was my "best friend" at the time, which presumably is why I was chosen. My friend lived down the Bay, so off I trotted. It was normal in those days for all front doors to be left open and you could see down the passageway into the kitchens of the houses. In one of the houses I passed there was a tiny puppy gambolling in the passageway. As this cute animal was irresistible to a small child, I walked into the passage to play with it. But when I bent over the pup I heard a bellow from further inside the house. The next moment a woman came running from the kitchen carrying a large knife. Once again I ran — out of the house and down the street with the woman galloping after me! Luckily she gave up the chase fairly quickly and I got back to school quite safely.

Of course, the woman might have been less vicious than she looked. Very likely she had been simply cutting a slice off the loaf and just came to investigate a strange child in her house, who was perhaps about to steal her puppy. But then again she could have been going to cut my head off!

Sam On Yen's was a well known Chinese restaurant in Bute Road. Local children used sometimes to annoy him by flinging open his door, yelling "Hullo Jesus," then slamming the door shut and running away. They used to say his name was, in fact, Jesus. The children found this very funny.

I never took part in this game. The first time I went to Sam On Yen's was as an adult when I went with a group of friends for

18

Ernest with his mother, Hannah on the left and his grandmother, Mary Housley on the right.

a meal. There were embroidered pictures around the walls which is the only thing I now remember about it though I'm sure we enjoyed the meal.

We lived with my grandmother (Hannah) and her two unmarried children, Ernest and Doris, in North Church Street. My uncle Ernest had various jobs — from barber's apprentice to pushing his own barrow round the streets selling vegetables. He finally settled for some years in the Sailor's Rest (British Sailors' Society) in Bute Road as a steward. He went on from there to be in charge, at different times, of British Sailors' Society hostels in Newport, Bristol and Avonmouth. Later on he moved to the Missions to Seamen with whom he did the same job.

Ernest was a very kindly man. Some time in the thirties, he married a lady called Fanny Veale. They never had children of their own but every school holiday one or more of their nieces and nephews would be invited to spend a week or more with them, wherever they were living.

Auntie Doris worked as a machinist in the Co-operative Wholesale Society (CWS) shirt factory which was then in Bute Terrace. She was a vivacious, jolly person who seemed always

Co-operative Wholesale Society shirt factory, Bute Terrace, outing 1920's. Doris McCluskey in charabanc at back immediately to the left of the wall drain pipe.

to be giggling. She must have been about twenty two when I was born and I was about six when she married.

When I was seven years old one of the traumatic incidents of my life occurred. Auntie Doris suddenly appeared with a baby girl. Where it had come from was one of life's mysteries. None of the adults appeared to know or, if they did, they weren't telling. The baby was to be called Marita and where the name came from was another of the mysteries.

She was duly christened at St Mary's Church by Father Thomas, who bent down to me and asked what I thought of the new little doll I now had. I replied indignantly that this was a baby not a doll. How could a grown-up not realise that?

I was quite put out by the arrival of Marita as I had been the youngest of all the cousins up until then. Still, she settled in remarkably quickly and it was as if she had never not been so to speak. Their family home was in Ely but they visited a lot, so I now had my own family baby to mind — and minded she was, complete with the usual mad dashes on top of the pram.

Marita was very good. She didn't cry much when we skidded round corners. She merely opened her eyes wider and gave the impression that, had her arms been longer, she would have grasped the sides of the pram.

When Marita grew older and was able to get around on her own we once lost her for several hours during which the family and various neighbours ran frantically round in circles looking for her. We were by now living in Pomeroy Street and some neighbours (and my Nana) insisted that she was probably in the river and half-way to Bristol by now. But another neighbour eventually knocked at the door with news. Marita was under the table (which was, of course, covered by the usual long fringed chenille tablecloth) in her house and refusing to come out. I was consequently sent to haul her from the hiding place.

Two other cousins arrived after Marita but they didn't have the same shock value as Marita had. I was used to mysterious babies by then.

Mother eventually gave up tailoring: perhaps a full-time job was too difficult with us children to care for. She did part-time cleaning work at the Sailors' Rest and later on at various offices and cinemas.

Chapter Two

Houses Where We Lived

The sort of shared household in which we grew up was a fairly common way of living at that time. Most people rented accommodation. Few bought houses — at least in our circles. A lot of young married people would rent "rooms" in someone else's home. ("Rooms" usually meant one room downstairs and one room upstairs and the shared use of kitchen and bathroom — if any!) Some people brought up their families under those kind of conditions. We were lucky in that our shared household consisted only of family.

At first we lived in North Church Street — Number 17. Later we moved to Pomeroy Street, in the bottom end of Butetown.

Number 17 North Church Street was a six-roomed terrace house. It stood last but one in the terrace. On one side lived the Sweeneys, who were last in the terrace. On the other were the Plaidy's and then Mrs Mosiach, who was an old lady living on her own. On the other side of the street lived the Mahoneys next door to the Glamorgan Hotel. The Mahoney and Sweeney children were our playmates, together with the Saunders children who lived higher up the street.

As you entered the dark green front door of 17 North Church Street the stairs faced you at the end of the passage. The *sanctum sanctorum* (i.e., the front room) was through the first door on the left. The furnishings of the *sanctum sanctorum* included the horse-hair sofa, the aspidistra plant in the window (covered by heavy lace curtains tied back to the walls) and the gramophone. The gramophone was a large square wooden box with a lifting lid and little doors at the front from where the sound came. Some of the records I remember were "The Teddy Bears

Picnic," "Red Sails in the Sunset" and "Oh for the Wings of a Dove" (with a boy soprano singing). The last of these was my Grandmother's favourite.

On the walls were three pictures. Two were a matched pair, *Before the Trial* and *After the Trial*, a set of Victorian prints which "told a story." The third picture was an oil painting of a landscape, which had a castle in the distance and cattle at the front.

The mantelpiece, of course, had its ornaments. Amongst other items, these included two large pale bluey-green vases with flowers painted on them. As you would expect, there was a mirror over the mantel.

Coming out of the front room and turning left you went around a corner at the foot of the stairs and through a door into the middle room. This was the room in which we customarily lived.

There was a window looking out into the backyard and a big fireplace with a high mantelpiece to the edge of which was fastened a velvet hanging the width of the mantel and probably about eight inches deep. White swans were embroidered along the velvet and at the bottom were bobbles.

The fireplace itself had an oven on either side of it in which my Grandmother sometimes put things to cook. On the floor in front of the fireplace was a cast iron fender with a complicated curly pattern at the front. Before the fender in front of the fire was a rag rug made from tailors' samples given to my Nana by a Packman (a travelling salesman).

In the fender immediately in front of the fire itself was a cast iron "stand" and under the stand in the fender lay the poker, tongs and shovel. All this black cast iron, the fire bars, the ovens, the fender, stand and so on were polished every day with "blacking" when the grate was cleaned and a new fire lit.

There were wooden armchairs on either side of the fire covered with blue and black quilted covers made by my Grandmother. There was a table in here as well back against the wall opposite the fire usually but pulled out when the family sat round it to eat. When not laid for meals the table would be covered with a large plush cloth. The table with the cloth over made a lovely cave for we children to hide under and play!

Down the flagstoned passage again and you were in the kitchen. Against one wall of the kitchen were built-in shelves beneath which was a long-legged marble-topped table. The table had drawers immediately below the marble top and a shelf about four inches from the floor.

Outside the back kitchen door were two or three steps down to the yard and opposite the kitchen was a small washhouse with a doorway (no door) and an unglazed window. Inside the washhouse, in a corner, was a boiler where the clothes would be boiled every Monday. If Monday happened to be rainy, the wet clothes would also be dried in the washhouse. The ironing was done on the table in the middle room which would be covered with a blanket kept specially for the purpose. The irons were black metal ones heated on the fire and used in pairs: one iron would be on the fire heating whilst the other was being used and then they were swapped over as the one in use became cool. Thick quilted holders were made with which to pick up the iron by the handle as it would be too hot to touch with your bare hand.

Carrying on down the back yard was the garden which always had flowers. One wall was covered with white jasmine and at the bottom of the yard beside the backdoor was a small rockery.

The toilet was at the end of the backyard. This was a small brick building with a wooden seat right along the back. Yes, there were drains! But there was no flush tank above. The toilet was flushed with buckets of water so that whenever it was used a bucket of water had to be washed down it and the bucket immediately filled once again in the kitchen and returned to the toilet.

There was a back door at the end of the yard which opened into Greek Church Street.

Upstairs in the house were three bedrooms. There was no bathroom. Bathing took place in a large zinc bath in front of the middle room fire, the water being boiled on the gas stove in the kitchen and carried through together with cold water in case it was too hot. Bathing in front of the fire was really very cosy especially on a cold winter day! The towel would be draped over the fireguard. The only problem as far as I was concerned as a child was that my brother and I were usually bathed together and

Francis and Phyllis aged about five and three.

25

he, as the eldest, would be attended to first, so by the time I was reached the towel would be wet and soggy.

At the top of the stairs were three or four steps going down to the back bedroom which had a window overlooking the backyard. Going towards the front of the house there was a bedroom above the downstairs middle room and a large bedroom at the front of the house over the front room and also covering the front part of the downstairs passage.

On the landing before entering the front bedroom there was a large cupboard.

As a very small child I slept in the same room as my parents. My father, who did all the decorating, once did the room in pale bluish grey. Around the bottom of the walls just above the skirting was a paper border of sea waves and scattered here and there over the wallpaper were paper seagulls of various sizes to give an impression of distance which were stuck on to the walls after the painting was finished.

The front bedroom was occupied by my Great Grandmother, my Grandmother and my Aunt. The back bedroom was occupied by my Uncle and my brother.

I was four years old when my Great Grandmother died (she was ninety two years of age). She had made her daughter, my Grandmother, promise to have only horses at her funeral — none of these new-fangled motor carriages! This was in 1934 so I suppose hers might have been one of the last horse-drawn funerals of the Twentieth Century. There were black horses with great ostrich feather plumes at their heads. Mourners followed the horse-drawn hearse in horse-drawn carriages. I didn't attend this funeral, being so small, but I remember standing at the front door and seeing all the horses in the street.

The house at Pomeroy Street never seemed so cosy as the North Church Street house. It was an end house next door to the corner shop and seemed to be just pushed in as a makeweight on the row.

The inside of the house was painted dark green — probably a job lot bought by the landlord.

It was narrower than the other houses in the terrace BUT it had a bathroom! This was a very small room at the top of the stairs just big enough to hold a bath and a small wash basin. The water was heated by a gas geyser which always lit with an enormous bang and then hissed and groaned loudly whilst the water ran. But the water was hot — very hot!

An awful and terrifying incident happened in this bathroom when we were children. My brother was having a bath and had the geyser running whilst he was in the bath. It was a very old geyser and very little fresh air entered the bathroom. We heard a loud bump and ran upstairs. The door was bolted from the inside. My father banged on the door and called out but there was no reply. Somehow he managed to break open the door. There was my poor brother in the bath unconscious, overcome by the fumes from the geyser. He was lifted out and put into bed where, once taken from the bathroom atmosphere, he recovered fairly quickly. And, I am glad to say, he is still with us to this day.

After that the window was repaired and was always left open when anyone was in the bathroom — winter as well as summer!

The kitchen of this house was overrun with blackbeetles. We seemed always to be putting down borax to kill them but they didn't really go until years later when I removed the old wash boiler in the scullery and found the nest. Oh! horrible! But a few kettlefuls of boiling water solved the problem.

In this house the coalhouse was in the kitchen! There was nowhere else to keep coal. The backyard was minute: half the size of the one in North Church Street and half-filled with a shed which my father used.

The toilet in this house was also in the backyard. This one, however, had a proper flush.

Chapter Three

CAMPBELL'S STEAMERS,
THE BRISTOL CHANNEL AND FLAT HOLM

In the 1930s Uncle Ernie had two bell tents at Lavernock, probably in the same field where today there are caravans. One of the tents was used for daytime living and the other for sleeping. We children would be taken there for a few days' holiday in the summer and this would be a wonderful, almost exotic, time: it was so out of the ordinary.

In the evenings gramophones could be heard over the camp and banjos would be strummed whilst the campers sang.

Several members of the family would be present and sometimes we would be accompanied by Ernie's friends. They always seemed to be seamen with strange and interesting tales to tell.

My elder cousins, Donald, John and June, would get up games of cricket. Or more probably baseball — their father, Alec Munro, having been a well known baseball player in his young days.

Alec Munro and Eliza McCluskey on their wedding day.

28

Eliza Munro, at the back with Mary Housley holding John Munro on the left and Hannah McCluskey holding Donald Munro on the right.

I was always put to field and would usually end up sulking since I never got to bat or bowl. (I probably was too small and insignificant!) If the others were all "out" and my turn seemed to be approaching, tea-time seemed always to be arriving even faster. And so I would end up gloomily sulking over a piece of bread and butter (instead of the daisy chains I made whilst "fielding").

There was a farm shop in the field with a very high counter. The person behind the counter would always call small children to the front to be served first — assuming you could remember what you had been sent to fetch!

The beach was reached down a steep cliff path and we thought ourselves very brave as we made the first step over to go down to the beach. There was one occasion when a triangular fin was sighted in the sea and a cry of "Sharks!" went up. Adults ran from the sea snatching up children as they ran and other adults ran down the beach to grab their children out of the sea. Once out we all stood, breathless, gazing at the sea, looking for the fin. Some cried, "There it is, there it is!" But I never saw it and so I felt cheated.

Sometimes my father would take us to Sully where he would prise limpets from the rocks then light a fire on the beach and cook the limpets for us to eat. I can't remember now what they tasted like but I suppose like any other seafood.

When my Uncle Ernie (who was now married) had his own Sailors' Rest — "over the water" in Bristol — all his nephews and nieces were invited in turn to visit him and his wife. Of course, the travelling was done usually by Campbell Steamer from the Pier Head. The journey itself was an adventure. You walked down the slipway on to the pontoons, which would bob and jig a little under the weight of the people boarding the ship, and then on to the ship itself. Usually there would be more than one boat going to various destinations: Minehead, Ilfracombe, Bristol and Weston. There was no holding us children once on board! Round the deck several times and then down to see the engines! Great pistons thudding to and fro sending the paddles churning round, the water turning into white billows behind the paddle wheels.

In those days you would occasionally see porpoises in the

Campbell's Steamer, Glen Usk, leaving Cardiff probably 1950s.

Bristol Channel. People would rush to the side of the ship from where the porpoises could be seen and the boat would heel over in the water. The boats would be very full of people on most trips. It seemed as though wet or fine weather people went to Weston or Bristol or Ilfracombe.

Every year Uncle Ernie went to some kind of celebration on the Flat Holm — I think there was a pub there at that time. Uncle Ernie belonged to a Society. He never told us what it was all about — perhaps it was a secret society. (As I said, I don't know what the Society was about but in recent years I've been told it could have been to do with Trinity House.)

Chapter Four

THE THIRTIES' DEPRESSION
AND CLOTHES FROM MRS KITCHEN

I remember little of the effects of the Depression of the 1930s. Perhaps, living with my family, there was always someone working and the money would be used for the whole household. Also, my grandmother had the Old Age Pension of ten shillings. (fifty pence) and a second pension of ten shillings. from the death of a son, Alfred John McCluskey, in the Great War. This was the son who had gone to live in Australia in his teens and, with the War, joined the Tenth Australian Light Horse. He was killed at Gallipoli. He was — and still is! — one

Alfred John McCluskey.

of my heroes. I still possess one of his spurs and his Sergeant's stripes and a medal. We used to have his sword — but that sadly disappeared somewhere, some time.

I remember once asking my mother for a halfpenny (old money) to buy a bar of chocolate and not understanding why she burst into tears.

Perhaps we two children were well-cushioned from the effects of the Depression. Perhaps if we did feel the effects of the Depression I have forgotten and remember only the happy parts.

My Mother made our clothes at that time. There was an old lady living across the street from us, Mrs Kitchen, who was well-off. She used to "dress" for her evening dinner. Having dined, she'd come to our house — very décolleté — for a chat. My Aunt Doris was then in her late teens or early twenties, and a joyful flapper! Mrs Kitchen would complain about the briefness of young womens' clothing and Doris would come back about the necklines of old ladies! It was all friendly though and years later Doris took her children to visit Mrs Kitchen.

Mrs Kitchen had a maid, whose name I forget, but who

Phyllis Rose Grogan, aged about seven.

Francis Henry Grogan, aged about eight.

was a great chatterbox. The old lady would send over her "old" clothes for my mother to make over for us, and the maid would help. Many a time I stood on a table being pushed and pulled this way and that by Mrs Kitchen's maid with pins sticking in various parts of my body but exhorted to "Keep *still!* There's a good girl!" She seemed to hold an endless supply of pins in her mouth, snatching more and more out and thrusting them into the garment I wore. I used to shudder to imagine the pins being swallowed!

Chapter Five

MEALS

Meals seemed to be the same from one week to another. Sunday was roast meat with potatoes, cabbage or broccoli, swede or carrots. On Monday (washing day) we had Sunday's leftovers. Other meals would be sausages stewed with tomatoes and onions and eaten with mashed potato; pease pudding with cold meat and bottled tomato sauce; fish with peas, potatoes and parsley sauce; and, as an occasional supper dish, sprats.

I never tasted mushrooms until I grew up, nor real cream. We had cream buns now and again but the "cream" was not the real thing.

My grandmother, who did all the cooking and housekeeping, was a good cook. Probably this was because she worked as a cook in her young days. She did not learn to read nor write until she reached her sixties and so her recipes were all in her head.

When she finally did learn to read all the reading she did was the daily *South Wales Echo* and *The Bible*. I never knew her to have any trouble with reading considering she learned so late in life.

Chapter Six

CHRISTMAS TIME

Christmas was a wonderful time.

It started with my grandmother making the puddings, which she mixed in a huge bread crock (a great lidded earthenware container where normally the bread was kept). The smell was fantastic — sweet, spicy, boozy! There was nothing like Christmas pudding for delicious smells! Each member of the family had to stir, three times clockwise, and then make a wish — but you must tell no one your wish, because if you tell the wish will never come true! When the ceremony of stirring was over the mixture would be ladled into basins with white cloths tied over the top. A fire would have already been lit under the water-filled copper in the washhouse and the puddings would be boiled for hours, finally being taken out and turned upside down round the edge of the copper to drain. There was one pudding for each of Grandmother's married children, one for us at home and another for New Year's Day. There would also be a small one — a "taster" — to be eaten on the day they were cooked. To this day, I've never tasted puddings like my grandmother's. They were sublime!

In our house the decorations and the tree went up on Christmas Eve — never before. This job was done by the adults, with us children "helping." The wooden stepladder would be brought in from the backyard shed and my father would place it in a corner of the room and demand the end of the first garland (all coloured paper — no foil). One of us would take a garland from the dusty cardboard box where they lived all the rest of the year and carry it carefully to the corner. Father would take the end of it and the rest would open out and concertina to the floor. I would be wild with the excitement of seeing the bright colours swaying from the ceiling!

Two rooms would be decorated, the back room where we lived and ate most of the time and the holy of holies, the front room, where the Christmas Party would be held.

The tree would be erected in the front room and decorated with glass baubles kept from year to year. In later years, it would be hung with electric fairylights in the shape of lanterns, gnome-like figures, stage coaches, candles, etc.

A fire would be lit in the fireplace of the bedroom where we children slept and we would doze off in the flickering firelight: it was the cosiest feeling in the world. Stockings would have been hung downstairs above the big fireplace. You would wake on Christmas morning to the feeling of being somehow crowded in bed. Putting my nose over the bedclothes I would dimly see something at the foot of the bed. A doll? Books? A box of — what? There can never be excitement as intense as the excitement of a child's Christmas morning!

It would be far too early to go downstairs — and probably too dark to see whatever was to be seen. Packages left at the foot of the bed would be fingered and even smelt for clues as to their contents. They would all be opened long before the adults were awake and moving. Then downstairs there would be more surprises in the stockings — nuts and tangerines in the toes and small toys and sweets filling the rest.

Christmas Dinner would be a party in itself. The aunts, uncles and cousins would be all crowded round the table in the middle room. There were bright-coloured crackers on the table to be pulled — a bit frightening when they "banged" but paper hats, jokes and a tiny present would drop out as they ripped open. Everyone wore a paper hat and the jokes and mottoes would be read out to shrieks of laughter. I always seemed to be puzzled: I would laugh with everyone else but secretly wondered what was so funny?

Later, we would all move into the front room where there

would be nuts, figs, dates, sweets and marzipan figures made by my father. Some of the sweets would be home-made too: I still have the recipe book which they used.

There would be more presents under the tree — some of them brought by the visiting relations, others left by us for them. Opening these presents was always a great ceremony. My father would pick up a present and hand it to the person to whom it was addressed who would then open it so we could all see and admire — or not as the case might be! Then on to the next present and next person, which could be himself.

I remember one dreadful Christmas when every present given to my father was a tie! I never knew whether this was accidental or some kind of joke but every time he opened another parcel containing a tie his face grew redder and his manner more abrupt until he finally exploded. I think one of the uncles then took over responsibility for handing-out!

After the presents there would be games and/or my father, who fancied himself as a conjurer, would give a show. Since I was the youngest I would usually be asked to "Pick a card" or "Hold the end of this ordinary piece of string." I became even more bewildered than I had been over the cracker jokes! I never seemed to understand the point of the tricks. I never knew *what* had disappeared or *where*. More important, I could never figure out *why?* What was the point of having one little red ball which became two, three or four little red balls and then having all the little red balls disappear? Weren't balls meant to be bounced or thrown? Once vanished I never saw them again. As as far as card tricks were concerned, I merely grew irritated and might end up crying if expected to see too many ladies disappear.

Usually we children would wander off to the back room to play with our new toys and leave the grown-ups and older cousins to their strange goings-on in the front room. I'm still not too happy at parties, still confused at what it's all about!

Chapter Seven

ST DAVID'S DAY

St David's Day was always a big day at school. In the morning there would be a concert performed by the children, and then, of course, the obligatory half-day in the afternoon. For the concert we would do tiny plays and little dances and songs. Generally our outfits would be made by our mothers from coloured crêpe paper. We would be dressed as daffodils or some other flower — but mostly it was daffodils because this is Wales after all and the daffodil is the national flower!

Phyllis Rose Grogan, dressed for a St. David's Day concert, 1938.

At one concert I was decked out as a gypsy in a cotton outfit sewn by my mother, complete with a basket of new pegs. Afterwards I was taken to a photographer who posed me, arms akimbo, one foot pushed forward. "Lift your chin and smile!" he cried, but I was tired of the whole thing and rather embarrassed.

There was one child who attended ballet lessons out of school. She did a little dance dressed in a tutu and point shoes, lifting her arms above her head. I was totally entranced by all this.

At one concert — but I think it must have been an Empire Day concert rather than a St David's Day one — I had to learn a speech which had been made by the King, George V, to the children of the Empire. Standing on a chair between two of the "big" boys, who stood on the floor on either side of my chair holding a Union Jack over my head, I had to repeat the speech to the assembled school. As this was during the reign of George V, I would have been five years old or less.

Chapter Eight

WHITSUN TREAT AND OTHER OUTINGS

Each Whitsun the Sunday School children were given a "Treat". This meant we were taken "to the country" — which, in our case, usually meant a field not very far away. We would go in lorries loaned by various traders in which benches had been placed. We would be lifted or would scramble up on to the back of the lorries and off we'd go! There was no shelter from the rain but in those far off days it never seemed to rain! If it occasionally did it seemed hilarious to us.

At the field there would be sideshows such as Hoop-la, coconut shies, etc. Perhaps they would be supplied by fairground people (I don't know if that was so) or perhaps they were put up by the organisers (I think that is more likely).

There would also be races — three-legged races, sack races or straightforward running according to your age. Some-

St. Mary's Church Whitsun Treat. Phoebe Saunders sitting furthest left, then Phyllis and Francis Grogan in front row.

times there would be competitions for the young men — greasy pole fights, for instance.

Then there would be tea and buns for refreshment, and at the end of the day we would all climb or be lifted back on to the lorries for the ride back. As Whitsun is in April or May, dusk could be falling as we drove back. It was a great adventure to be out in the dark on strange roads!

My mother used to talk of Whitsun Treats to which she went as a girl in Cathays Park — where the Civic Centre now stands. Apparently, there was a long tradition of these outings.

Besides Whitsun Treats there were, occasionally, other outings. Mr Sweeney (husband of the lady with the shop mentioned later) once owned a car — something very unusual in our circles — and he once took all the children in North Church Street out for the day. I was the smallest child at that time

Mothers' Meeting outing from St. Mary's Church in the twenties. Hannah Louisa McCluskey, centre back with black hat.

and my own little stool was placed on the floor of the back of the car for me to sit on. The other children squashed up on the back seat or sat on the floor. There must have been arms and legs sticking out of every window. We went towards Cowbridge and picnicked on the Common. Unfortunately, on the way back, the car broke down and all of us had to get out and push!

We did get back home — somehow or other.

My father was a great one for walking. He would take Polly and us children on long, long hikes up over Leckwith Hill and down into Ely (which wasn't as built up as it is now). Or into Dinas Powys or Barry. We would be shown all the wild flowers and made to learn their names and then tested when we got home as to what we remembered.

It didn't do too much good: I remember the names of very few wild flowers!

Chapter Nine

THE GREEK CHURCH, ST. MARY'S CHURCH AND THE VICAR

In those days at Easter the priests of the Greek Church would distribute coloured hard-boiled eggs to the children of the district. We would all cluster round the doorsteps of the Church whilst the priest, bearded and tall-hatted, handed eggs out to us. I don't remember ever eating them — probably the colours were too pretty to spoil.

Our own church was St Mary's Church. I and most of my family were christened there and my mother was married there during the first World War — at eight o'clock in the morning, so I was always told. Perhaps Harry, who would have been in the Army at the time, was on a short leave and the wedding was pushed in at probably the only time possible. My family was a

The altar of St. Mary's Church.

44

St. Mary's Church Scouts in the twenties. Henry James Ambers-Grogan, middle row second from left.

church-going family and my brother and I were taken or sent twice — sometimes I seem to remember three times — every Sunday. We went to Sunday School as well.

The Vicar at that time was Father Garland and his curate was Father Thomas. Both were very tall big men — or perhaps it was just that I was small! Mrs Garland sat just behind us in church, singing all the hymns loudly in a very deep contralto voice. Both Father and Mrs Garland frightened me to pieces. It was not because they were ever unkind. More likely it was because they seemed so large and so distant.

My brother also sang in the church choir as a small boy.

My Grandmother was a church cleaner, so we were well-known to the Garlands. My brother (Francis) and I also went to the schools belonging to the Church. Father Garland would visit the schools from time to time. I distinctly remember him visiting my class. At some point during his visit, he would look round the class and see me. Stretching out his arm, he'd point to me and beckon. I would have to get up and creep to the front of the class where he would proceed to question me as to the health of my family, particularly my grandmother (Mrs Hannah McCluskey).

45

This recurrent ordeal terrified me! The sound of Father Garland's voice in the corridor would set me shaking and I would shake for some time after he left. I'm sure he had no idea and meant only kindness.

Chapter Ten

MRS SWEENEY'S, STREET TRADERS AND SHOPS.

Miss Steadman the Babies' Class teacher was a lovely lady. She was fond of her little ones and used to buy us sweets quite often. One of us would be sent to Mrs Sweeney's shop down the street (next door to our house) for a bag of "fishes" which would then be shared amongst the class. "Fishes" were boiled sweets, fruit drops I suppose, which were in the shape of fish.

Mrs Sweeney's "shop" was not a shop in the manner of today's shops. It was simply her front room, with a table serving as a counter. As far as I remember, Mrs Sweeney sold basics such as flour and tea as well as sweets, but all in small quantities.

Milk and bread were delivered — well not exactly delivered. The milkmen came round the streets with a "float," a kind of small hand cart with a milk churn suspended in it. He would call "O-lao-o-laity" (or something like that) and people would come from the houses with their own containers — milk jugs, whatever. He would fill these by using his "measures" and dipping into the churn. The measures were metal containers shaped something like a straight sided mug with a hooked handle at the top and came in varying sizes — pint, half pint, gill (quarter pint). The hooked handle

Milk float with churns.

47

was to hang them either somewhere about the cart or over the lip of the churn.

Bakers came in a high, horse-drawn cart. The cart was small but covered and lofty. Again, people would come from the houses to buy.

Other traders came. *Fishmongers* (Tommy-the-Fish being the one most of the people in our area remember), *greengrocers*, *knife-grinders* — all these with handcarts. The *salt-and-vinegar men* came with a horse-drawn cart. As for the *rag-and-bone men*, some had horses while others pushed handcarts. The rag-and-bone man would take all sorts of rags or old clothes. In exchange he would give a child's toy — a balloon mostly I think or perhaps a windmill, one of those twisted paper ones on sticks.

There were plenty of shops, of course, but street trading was very common. Oh! I almost forgot *the ice cream man!* At that time he too was horse-drawn, in a van almost like a gypsy caravan but not so high. Dimascio's is the name that comes to mind. There were also *Wall's Stop-me-and-Buy-One men* on tricycles with big box-like containers at the front. There would be wafers for the adults and cornets for the children or ice lollies (not called ice lollies at that time but the name I forget) from Walls — triangular sticks of fruit flavoured icy stuff wrapped in paper, very similar to some of today's treats. In town in the winter there would be *hot chestnut men*, with their little barrows consisting of a glowing brazier where they cooked the chestnuts and a container for cooked and uncooked nuts.

Chapter Eleven

1d FOR THE METER

Before the mid to late 1930s the house was lit by gas. Over the fireplace in every room there was a gas bracket with a glass shade covering the gas mantles. The gas would hiss softly as it burned and gave a gentle, warm, yellow light. Gas came through a 1d-in-the-slot meter. As the 1d ran out, the light would begin to flicker and there would be a mad scramble to get to the meter with another 1d before the light went out. If it did go out before the meter was reached you had to be sure to turn the gas off before you put the 1d in, because the gas would start to flow immediately and could be dangerous, especially so in a room with an open coal fire.

Schools were also lit by gas. There were great four-armed crosses with a globe on each arm descending from the ceiling. They were lit by means of pulling at chains hanging from them.

School gas light.

Chapter Twelve

ST. MARY'S SCHOOL

My first school, St Mary's Bute Road, was Infants and Girls only. I went to Infants at St Mary's and continued there in what was then called Elementary School — in other words, Junior or basic school.

The first teacher I remember was Miss Steadman. She was the teacher for the Babies' Class (i.e., the class for the very youngest children). I went to school at the age of three, as did many other children. I could already read and write, having been taught at home, my brother and I being only two children in a house of five adults. We (two children and our parents) lived with my grandmother who still had two unmarried children at home. So, as small children we were never short of attention, including a bit of informal schooling.

Because St Mary's was an Infants' School and a Girls' Elementary School, my brother, Francis, had to leave when he finished Infants at seven years of age. He had to go to Bute Terrace School which was "Mixed" (Boys and Girls).

Where classes were "mixed" boys sat on one side of the room and girls on the other. Recalcitrant children were sometimes punished by making them sit amongst those of the opposite sex where other class members would jeer at them!

If the class was noisy or misbehaving we might all be made to sit with our hands on top of our heads for a while or with our hands behind our backs.

There was one visiting priest (we had such people during Lent) who had a rather odd habit. He would stride up and down in front of the class with his hands behind his back holding a blackboard duster (one of those felt-covered wooden blocks). Then suddenly without warning he would turn to face us and would hurl the block into the class. Every desk cover would fly up as all the children crouched down behind them! I don't think we ever learnt anything from him, except to watch for signs indicating he was about to turn and hurl!

The school teachers at St Mary's were Miss Steadman, Miss Jarrold, Miss Miller, Miss Planck and Miss Harrison, the Head Teacher. Miss Planck was a German lady. When the war started she, sadly, was interned in a prison camp, as were all German nationals at that time. My grandmother told us to pray for the poor soul but I was never a believer in God.

When I was a young child all the teachers seemed old. I now realise that some of them were young. Miss Jarrold was a young lady who wore her hair in two plaits. They were rolled to the sides of her head over her ears to form "telephones". She was a very kind person, who, like several of these teachers, seemed fond of the children she taught.

Miss Miller had been a missionary in, I believe, South America. She was a great King Arthur fan and told us knightly tales. She was still living ten or fifteen years ago (it's 1994 as I write this), residing in St Mary's vicarage.

Miss Harrison was a more distant figure. This was probably because she was the Head Teacher and responsible for disciplining children who had committed more serious offences — such as when my desk-mate and I (we sat in "paired" desks) carved Union Jacks on the top of the desk. "What if everyone did that?" she scolded. I thought, "Wouldn't it make the desks less plain? Wouldn't it make them more interesting?" But I didn't dare say that!

We used to have swimming lessons on those desks — dry-land swimming. We would be told to lie across the desktops and wave our arms and legs about "like a frog", the teacher would call, "Like a frog". We were all dedicated townies and probably none of us had ever set eyes on a real frog but we tried all the same. "Breathe!" she would order "Breeeeathe!" I don't think

51

any of us had really stopped breathing — still we puffed loudly to please her.

Sewing was one of the subjects taught at school. You started very young with "useful" stitches — tacking, running stitch, darning, etc. The big girls made articles of clothing for "the orphans". I never found out who "the orphans" were and wonder sometimes if they appreciated the petticoats made for them. I never reached the stage of sewing for the orphans because we moved house and I had to go to a different school (Clarence Road) where embroidery rather than useful sewing was taught.

Each Christmas at St Mary's, Bute Road there would be a Christmas Party. One year the teachers decided it would be a fancy dress party, with each child coming in his or her national dress. Now, this was Tiger Bay and there were children of all nations living there. I was almost ashamed of being just a British child with no unique national dress. I had a new skirt and jumper but that was nothing like as interesting as the others. Particularly the Arab and Chinese girls decked in bright colours — some with gold coins attached to the edge of their jackets or golden and brightly coloured braids stitched to their garments and bangles round their ankles and arms.

Because St Mary's, Bute Road was a Church school and only just over the road from the church, we were taken quite frequently *en masse* to St Mary's Church. On certain saint's days and church festivals we would go to church in the mornings and, of course, there would be a half-day off in the afternoon.

Through Lent we were taken to church every Wednesday morning and given a lecture by a visiting priest. In the case of one particular priest, this lecture took the form of a description of a particular sin as if it were a wicked giant. The priest had big pictures of these giants which he hung up before us. Poor giants! Spotted, ugly, lame, misshapen! I felt they should be looked after rather than hated.

At that time as well as attending ordinary school the Muslim boys went to their own school one day a week where they were taught the Koran. There would be occasional processions of Muslims up Bute Road when they took some of their community to the railway station on the start of a journey to Mecca. I believe they collected money amongst themselves to send one or two each year.

An important part of the education in Tiger Bay was gained outside of books. We learned to appreciate other cultures.

Chapter Thirteen

CLARENCE ROAD SCHOOL

In about 1940 because of the many air raids parents were made to send their children to the schools closest to their homes. By now we were living in Pomeroy Street but still attending St Mary's School, Bute Road. This edict meant that I would now have to attend Clarence Road School in Hurman Street (incidentally right next door to a Currans, a munitions factory!).

I mentioned earlier that at St Mary's School we had dry-land swimming lessons — on our desktops. Well, at Clarence Road School we were taken weekly to Guildford Crescent baths to learn to swim in real water. We went two to a cubicle to change into our swimsuits and back again later, which was fine if you were both small but slightly inconvenient as we grew.

I was a non-swimmer at the time. Non-swimmers were left to play in the shallow end while the teacher coached those who could swim. At the end of the lesson all of us, swimmers and non-swimmers alike, had a diving lesson. Each child queued up to kneel at the edge of the pool, with arms stretched above head and head tucked firmly between arms. Then teacher placed her hand — or possibly her foot! — beneath the child's bottom and tipped him or her head-first into the water. This little exercise took place in the shallow end of the baths, so there was no danger of drowning. But it was a little disconcerting!

I didn't learn to swim until I was eighteen and long out of school.

At Clarence Road there was also the chance of Welsh lessons. For some reason, probably lack of time, the choice was between Welsh or History. My mother chose Welsh for me and off I went to learn Welsh. The teacher taught us little dances along with Welsh songs. She also translated some of the popular songs of the day into Welsh and taught us those, as well as trying to ram grammer into us. A teacher's lot is a hard one: I never learnt Welsh either.

Elementary school was, I think, mostly reading, writing and arithmetic. At eleven years of age you (or your parents!) chose whether or not to take an exam known then as The Scholarship. If successful, you went on to High (or Secondary) School. I don't know the proportion of children who went in for the exam or, of those, what number passed, but it seems to me that it wasn't such a lot. Children who were going in for the exam were taken out of the ordinary class and put into a special class called the Scholarship Class. While they were being coached not much was seen of them. They seemed almost like a group apart, like children with a special status.

I didn't go in for the Scholarship. I was not very fond of school and secondary education meant more years at school after the age of fourteen.

My husband (who was not a Docks boy) did go in for the Scholarship and passed it. However, he could never go to high school because his parents were unable to buy him the necessary uniform and equipment.

Chapter Fourteen

CENTRAL COMMERCIAL SCHOOL

At the age of twelve I was sent to the Central Commercial School in Frederick Street to learn shorthand and typing. My elder cousin, June, had become a shorthand typist — and everything that June did I also had to do, she being a kind of a heroine to me. If she was a typist then I had to be one. I've never been sure if it was really a good decision. However, at that time, the only employment choices for a girl were office, shop or factory work. My grandmother wanted me to go "into service" but this never appealed to me one bit having heard all her tales of servants' life.

The Central Commercial School was run by the three James sisters, Lillian, Sybil and a third sister who looked after the evening classes. (Since I didn't attend evening classes, I only knew Lillian and Sybil.) It was a very small school of two or three rooms only. Two rooms were classrooms and the third was for the sisters' own use.

Lillian was a good teacher and I learnt shorthand and typing very quickly from her, together with a certain amount of bookkeeping. The front room, facing on to Frederick Street, was the shorthand room and the back room was the typing room. For a time I was one of what Lillian called her "speed girls". The "speed girls" were those who had learnt the basics of shorthand and mainly needed to pick up some speed in writing it. So, whilst other girls were being taught the rules of shorthand in the front room, we would be sent to the back room to practise typing. Having mastered the keyboard, we would practise on our own — especially when Sybil, our typing teacher, was taking part in the teaching of shorthand.

Sometimes just one of us would type in order to make the

necessary sounds whilst the other two or three would chat or sneak out of the door and down the stairs to the snackbar next door to buy cartons of frozen fruit juice or buns.

The James sisters' father was a Channel pilot who had contacts in shipping offices round the docks. He would hear about job vacancies in the various offices he visited and would convey this information to his daughters, who would then send girls who were ready to go to work out for interviews. I found my first job in this way. It was with a company called Elder Dempster (Cardiff) Ltd.

Not the original Elder Dempster but a firm run by a man who had worked for Elder Dempster and had started his own shipping agency using the name of Elder Dempster with their permission. His name was Alfred Hogan and he was quite elderly when I went to work for him.

Mr Hogan's own room was furnished with a huge leather-topped desk and leather armchairs. When he and the other staff members were out I would go in his room and sit in the leather armchairs and fancy myself someone!

One of the other men working there was a Mr Silcox. He had lived in Marseille for many years working for Elder Dempster. When the war started in 1939 he had to make his escape, together with his wife and two children. They lost most of their belongings in the process.

The firm acted as agents for several shipping companies — Elder Dempster, Alfred Holt, Elders and Fyffes, Companie Maritime Belge and others. And the names of the ships were like poetry or a geography lesson — *Copacabana, Matadi, Takoradi.*

Chapter Fifteen

GAMES WE PLAYED

One of the games we played was *Aeroplanes*. You spread your arms wide and ran around making whirring, buzzing noises, imagining you were flying. In the 1930s planes were still exciting enough to have people running from their houses to look up if one passed over — adults as well as children!

We played *Mob* (hide and seek). We also played various kinds of *Touch*. There was of course the straightforward game where one person is "It" and chased the others until he or she managed to touch one of them, whereupon that person became "It" and did the chasing. Then there was *Touch Off the Ground*.

In Touch Off the Ground you couldn't be touched if your feet were off the ground. You could stand on a doorstep, jump on to a window sill, stand on a stone or brick and, if you were big enough, hang on a front door by clutching the knocker! You slid off that very easily though!

Also, there was *Touch on One Leg*. When "It" came near you stood on one leg and so could not be touched.

A variety of Mob (Hide-and-Seek) was called *Kick the Tin*. Instead of hiding his or her eyes and counting, the seeker, or one of the others, would kick a tin — an ordinary empty food can — as far as they could. The seeker would have to run and fetch the tin back to the starting point before commencing the search. There was a variant of Kick the Tin in which if one of the hiders could reach the recovered tin without being noticed he or she could then kick it away again. The poor seeker would have to go and fetch it back once more before continuing the search.

Another favourite pastime was *Whip-and-Top*. Tops came in various shapes with flat upper surfaces which we would decorate with coloured chalk so that as they spun round the colours would merge. The "whip" was about one foot long, the lash part being thin leather (I think).

Then there was *Hoops*. Most "hoops" were the frame of an old bicycle wheel with all the spokes removed and no tyre of course. You hit the hoop with a piece of stick to bowl it along. Or, in the absence of a stick, you used the flat of your hand, which resulted in many a sore hand. Hoops were amazingly noisy — imagine metal wheels over tarmac — and housewives would come out and berate us to go and play outside our own front door.

Girls played various games that involved either standing and doing various juggling things with a bouncing ball or bouncing a ball against the wall. There were about ten different ways of bouncing the balls in these games, which were called, of course, *onesees, twosees, threesees,* etc! Bigger girls played similar games but using two balls.

Skipping was also popular. It could be done either by a girl on her own or in groups. Skipping ropes for single skippers might have fancy handles with, perhaps, bells set in them (more noise!). For a group of girls you needed a long rope (perhaps someone's mother's washing line!). There were a variety of games to be played skipping either alone or in groups.

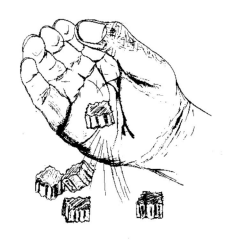

Gobs or *Fivestones* was another game which was played with five stones which might be dice-like as illustrated or simply pebbles or pieces of stone picked up

The game of Gobs, Jacks or Five Stones.

around the street. The game was played by holding all five stones in the hand and then tossing them in the air; as they came down you tried to catch them on the back of your hand. If none were caught you were "out" and the next child took a turn. If, however, you caught one or more you then had to pick up the remainder of the stones on the ground whilst retaining those on the back of the hand. If any were dropped you were "out". If you managed not to drop any the stones which were balanced on the back of your hand were tossed in the air with the object of catching them in the palm of your hand. If you didn't you were, once again, out!

Boys had games of their own and never played by girls. Their games involved things such as standing on one leg with the arms folded and hopping around trying to knock down the others. There was one game which ended with the loser having to run the gauntlet between two lines of boys and being punched, pinched or kicked all the way. There was a game called, I think, *Donkey*, where one boy stood bent over facing a wall with his hands against the wall, palms facing the wall and then the other boys would run at him from behind and leap on to his back. The boy had to stand as long as he could and the other lads had to cling on as long as they could. Real masculine stuff!

We also played round games such as *Ring-o-Roses* when we were little and, when we were getting older, *In and Out the Window*. These were called *Round Games*, because all the participants stood in a ring to play.

There was a ball game called *Queenie O Ko Ko* (honest!). One child stood with its back to a group of other children and flung a ball backwards over its shoulder. The others would try to catch it. If the ball was caught without bouncing the catcher would call "Queenie" and take her or his turn at the front to throw. If however the ball fell to the ground and had to be picked up then whoever picked it up hid it about her or his person and "Queenie" (the child at the front) had to guess who had it.

Children would shuffle together and pass the ball from one to another behind their backs to fool "Queenie".

There were one or two different ways of playing *Alleys* (or Marbles) — either along the gutter or with a chalked circle.

There were also games using cigarette cards (i.e., cards which used to accompany packages of cigarettes). As far as I can recollect some of these cards were propped against the wall while others were flicked at them to knock them over.

Then there was *Film Stars*. In this game someone would think of a film star and tell the others the star's initials. Then the others would try to guess the star.

Swinging was one of our childhood pleasures. We swung on lampposts. A rope was knotted into a large loop and flung over one of the projecting arms. Then you swung round and round the post until the rope was fully wound, whereupon you swung back again! Adults seemed to object strongly to this game — I suppose on the grounds that the rope could snap or even the lamppost might break. Needless to say, we continued.

There were also other opportunities for swinging. For example, makeshift swings were hung on front gate posts.

Cops and Robbers, Cowboys and Indians and, with the war, *English and Germans* — these games all semed to be much the same with everyone rushing around shouting "Bang, bang!"

We played *Shops, Schools* and *Hospitals*.

Swinging on the lamp-post.

61

Chapter Sixteen

THE CANAL, DIVERS AND THE TIMBER FLOAT

The Glamorganshire Canal used to run through the centre of the town. It entered the Bristol Channel via the sea-lock not far above the Hamadrayad Hospital and ran up into town parallel with Bute Road and then on to Merthyr. Many years ago, a sand dredger hit one of the lock gates and all the canal's water ran into the Bristol Channel. In Butetown the Glamorganshire Canal is now that long narrow green space running from St Mary's Church to below James Street. The part of the canal that ran through the town has long been built over. There's a memory of it in the name "Hayes Bridge Road". The "bridge" was a canal bridge.

We played alongside the canal as children and sometimes fished in it. Young lads would swim in it in the summer. Often they had no swimming costumes and swam naked. The canal crossed towards the Castle underneath Kingsway (the old tunnel is now a pedestrian crossing) and lads would swim in the canal where it surfaced behind the Rose and Crown.

There was a bridge there. People would lean over and throw pennies into the water for the boys who would dive into the canal for them. The lads would call up to the passers-by to throw their coppers.

Now and again there was the excitement of a professional diver in the canal. Divers went down, attached to a long rope, to clear mud and rubbish from around the lock gates. They wore rubber suits with great globular helmets and heavy clumpy boots. Attached to the helmet was an air pipe, which led from an air pump on the canal bank. The pump looked like a large box with a wheel at either end which had a handle jutting from it. Two men would stand at either end turning the wheels as long as the diver was down below. One of the men might allow you to grasp the pump handle sometimes, but not if the diver was down under the water.

The diver would enrobe himself in the diving suit on the canal bank. (The diving suits in those days were not the tight-fitting affairs worn now. They had a loose-ish fit.) He would then sit on the box in which the suit was kept whilst the other men placed the helmet over his head and screwed it down.

I always felt desperately anxious when the diver was under the black canal water. He seemed to stay down so long. I couldn't imagine how he could get out safely. It was always a huge relief when he came up again.

The locks themselves were fascinating. It seemed a daring and brave thing to cross the narrow plank bridges along their tops, especially if the lock water was low. You seemed to be standing on the edge of a cliff looking down.

There was death in the canal. Sometimes you would see a dog or cat, bloated, its four legs stiffly skywards, floating quietly down the canal and so out eventually to the Channel.

Some children died in the canal and so did some adults. I remember hearing of one poor man who wandered from the Old Sea Lock pub, slightly the worse for a few pints, and mistook his way in the dark. And once there was the dreadful sight of a severed human arm. The body to which it belonged never surfaced.

One or two children died over the years on the timber float — a large "lake" on which great baulks of timber were seasoned. Because the timber was massed on the float you could not see much water. Children, girls as well as boys, would dare each other to run over the wood. If a child slipped into the water between the planks the wood could then bump back together again. There would be no way up for the person trapped underneath.

Chapter Seventeen

MINDING YOUNG ONES

In those days girls were expected to look after small babies and other children younger than themselves. If we had no small babies in our own families we would tout around the neighbours to see if we could "mind" those. An older girl might hold the baby in her arms while an adult wrapped a large shawl around her and the baby. The shawl was generally fastened with a safety pin at the front, so the baby was effectively bound to the older child fairly safely. Sometimes, unfortunately, the pin came open, sticking the girl in the arm or the baby in the bum! This method of carrying babies was also used by adults and was called "Welsh fashion".

If the baby was in a pram, great! We could have a game, then. It consisted of running as fast as you could while pushing the pram. When the pram had a good head of steam in its wheels, perhaps if you were going downhill, then you would jump and fling yourself across the pram and ride it. I doubt if the mothers knew just what went on when they gave us their babies! On the other hand maybe they were too busy with other tasks to worry too much.

Chapter Eighteen

MEN'S GAMES AND RACING ANIMALS

On Sunday mornings some men would gather on wasteland away from the houses to play Pitch and Toss, a gambling game.

You would also see men standing at street corners whom other men and women would approach, speak to quickly while holding their hand — so I thought — and then hurry away. It was years before I learned what was really going on which was betting on horse racing. These men were called Bookies' runners and would carry the bets to the bookies.

Some men kept racing dogs which they exercised every day — tall beautiful greyhounds with huge dark eyes and emaciated-looking bodies. They always wore muzzles.

Racing pigeons were kept too and there was a family in Dumballs Road who bred budgies.

Chapter Nineteen

DOING OUR BIT FOR THE WAR

We gave little concerts, especially during the War, and charged the adults about 1d (an old penny) to come in. The money would then be given "for the War Effort" (as the saying was in those days). We also had little sales of any old junk we could find in our houses or cadge around the street, with the proceeds being "For the War Effort". One particular day two other children and I went with dozens of children from all over Cardiff to the Lord Mayor's Parlour with our contributions garnerned in such ways. He shook our hands, asked us how we got the money and thanked us.

There was also a campaign to persuade school children to save money for the war through Savings Stamps. If you took 6d (now two and a half pence) to school you were given a special certificate saying you had helped. Lots of us brought our 6d and got the certificates, but I can't say how many carried on saving, which, of course, was the idea. I only know I didn't. Pocket money was very sparse in those days!

When the war started my brother and I were in Bristol visiting relations. Living down the docks, we had gone by Campbell steamer rather than train: in the summer the boats went regularly to Bristol, among other places in Somerset and Devon. I think we must have come back on the day war was declared or the next day.

At that time Campbells docked at the Pier Head and upon disembarking you came up the slipway towards the Big Windsor. As we came within sight of the Big Windsor there was my grandmother. She was still wearing the big black apron that old ladies wore about the house but took off if they were going far beyond their own street. The apron was up over her head as she sobbed and cried under its cover because she thought the Germans would have torpedoed us in the Bristol Channel. Poor old lady, she must have been desperately upset, but I, at the age of 9, was only embarrassed.

A new game started with the air raids. It involved looking for pieces of shrapnel after a raid. We all became competitive over the number of pieces we found. Sometimes the shrapnel would be hot as you picked it up.

My brother and I were the proud possessors of an old postcard with a length of wire round it which was said to have come from the Graf Zeppelin in the Great War. It had been picked up by my father at the time the Graf Zeppelin came down. (The Graf Zeppelin was an airship — a dirigible — during the Great War of 1914-1918.) None of the other children ever beat that!

We made "museums" of such things and charged people to see them. All of the money collected went for "The War Effort". Adults must have been very long suffering!

My father was an Auxilliary fireman during the war. This meant that after he did his own full-time job — shift work in Currans, which was then a munitions factory — he went to the Fire Station and became a fireman for most of his "leisure" time. Other adults (mostly people who were too old for the armed forces or not healthy enough) did the same or became Air Raid Wardens.

The latter went round the streets making sure no one showed any lights from their houses. Everyone had thick black-out curtains and there were fines for "showing a light". (Towns were "blacked out" to make things difficult for German planes coming over to bomb us.) If there were no lights enemy aircraft couldn't see the towns too well. Moonlit nights were dreaded.

Vehicle headlights were covered with black shades leaving only slits of glass showing, and these were then painted blue to obscure yet more light. The windows of buses and tramcars

Henry James Ambers-Grogan in the uniform of the National Fire Service.

were painted over so little of the inside lights showed outside; and those inside lights themselves were painted over blue, which meant that they were very poorly lit inside. It was hard to tell where your stop was if you travelled at night since there were no street lights and the vehicles threw very little light into the darkness.

All the house windows had strips of brown paper criss-crossed over them. The idea was that if because of a nearby explosion the windows shattered, hopefully the paper would hold the glass together and so prevent injury from flying glass. At one time my father came home with special clear rubber-like paint to cover the windows. This paint served the same function as the brown paper and you didn't lose so much light with the paint as you did with the paper. However it smeared the window making it almost impossible to see out clearly.

There were plenty of daylight raids. At the height of the bombing, schools did not open until about eleven o'clock because of the constantly disturbed nights. We would go in at eleven and, for a while, everyone — teachers too — would swap experiences before starting classes. Then, with a bit of luck, there would be another air raid warning and school would finish for the day while we all scampered to shelter.

"Scampered" is the wrong word. We were walked in orderly files out of the class and down the stairs to the school shelter or, if you lived close, you were sent home.

In our street there was a lady, Mrs George, who kept a shop and had her basement reinforced to form an air raid shelter. She would be on the shop doorstep when the warning sounded ready to catch school children as they ran for shelter. We didn't need much catching as, once in her shelter, we were fed pop and biscuits.

Once during the war I had been given a new sliding pencil box for a birthday present. The warning sounded for a raid and we could already hear the planes as we walked down the stairs.

Suddenly — horror! — I remembered that my new pencil box was still on my desk top upstairs in the classroom! I instantly broke ranks and turned to pelt back upstairs again in order to fetch the box. No German bomb could be allowed to bomb that! Unfortunately for me the teacher, Miss Staniforth, thought I was panicking because of the noise of the raid and pelted after me. Having caught me she proceeded to shake me and smack my face hard — to stop what she thought was hysteria. I was dragged back downstairs again whilst the treasured box stayed up in the classroom. Luckily the school wasn't bombed that time. Indeed, it never was, even though it was next to Currans munitions factory.

My father shored up the basement under our house with pit props. We spent our nights sleeping down there instead of in the public shelter where many slept.

Some people had Anderson shelters in their back gardens. These were corrugated metal shelters which were half buried in the gound and covered by earth with flowers and vegetables planted on top. Some had Morrison shelters, which were like large metal cages and were kept in the house and used as a table. The idea was that if the house came down you in your shelter would be safe as the metal structure would hold the rubble away from you until you were dug out.

During the war we had very few sweets, nor fruit such as oranges or bananas since these came from overseas and food ships would be attacked and sunk by the enemy. Each person had a ration book — though I don't remember the quantities of foods allowed with the book — and there was also a sweet ration. My father took charge of the sweet ration for the whole family and usually bought treacle toffee as this was considered to be nutritious: Francis and I would be given one piece a day.

Chocolate was totally unobtainable until I went to work at Elder Dempsters. Ships (and I suppose soldiers and airmen) were given a ration of Cadbury's chocolate and sometimes the agents would bring a bar of chocolate each for the office juniors. Occasionally, towards the end of the war, ships started bringing in cargoes of oranges. Then the agents would give us presents of an orange.

These are some of my memories of childhood "down the Docks". I know things have changed a lot since those days.

LIFE STORIES FROM TIGER BAY

OUT NOW:

1. Neil M. C. Sinclair, M.A. :
   The Tiger Bay Story

2. Phyllis Grogan Chappell :
   A Tiger Bay Childhood: Growing Up in the 1930s

FORTHCOMING:

3. Harry Cooke ("Shipmate"):
   How I Saw It: Old Tiger Bay and the Docks

4. Olwen Blackman Watkins:
   A Family Affair: Three Generations in Tiger Bay

Series Editor: Glenn Jordan

5 Docks Chambers
Bute Street
Butetown
Cardiff CF1 6AG